Quic
What Authors ...

"Everything you need to know to write compelling short romances! Nancy Cassidy brings a wealth of experience as both an author and editor to this valuable resource." – Author Deborah Hale

"A practical and easy-to-read guide for writing short romantic fiction. Both beginning and experienced authors will appreciate the nuggets of information on how to craft a compelling short story." – Author Bev Pettersen

"*Quickies* reveals the ins and outs of writing short romance. As a new writer, it provides valuable advice in helping me be strategic in both my writing and marketing." – Aspiring Romance Author, G. Veronica Purcell

"The Short Plot Method in *Quickies* works with the writing basics as a useful tool to create short, enjoyable romances." – Author Cathryn Fox

QUICKIES:

WRITING SHORT FICTION FOR THE ROMANCE MARKET

Nancy Cassidy
TheRedPenCoach.com

QUICKIES:

WRITING SHORT FICTION FOR THE ROMANCE MARKET

A guide to writing and selling short stories to the romance market

Nancy Cassidy, The Red Pen Coach

QUICKIES: WRITING SHORT FICTION FOR THE MARKET
Copyright 2015 by Nancy Cassidy

Published by the Red Pen Coach
Edited by Pat Thomas
Cover by Jan Meredith

Quickies: Writing Short Fiction for the Romance Market
Discover more about writing with Nancy Cassidy
at **www.TheRedPenCoach.com**
A RedPenCoach publication

ALL RIGHTS RESERVED. This book contains material protected under International and Federal Copyright Laws and Treaties. Any unauthorized reprint or use of this material is prohibited. No part of this book may be reproduced or transmitted in any form or by any means, electronic or mechanical, including photocopying, recording or by any information storage and retrieval system without express written permission from the author/publisher.

First edition September 2015
ISBN print: 978-1-5175-7873-2

FOREWORD

So you have a great idea for a romance, but you want to keep it short? There's a large market today for short romantic fiction, especially in the virtual, electronic marketplace. People want to read something while they sit on the bus or ride the train to work. Something that is short, easy to read, but will make them feel good, the way romance novels do.

Keeping it brief without losing that level of emotional connection can be hard, but there are ways to make sure your book is a satisfying romance read, even with a limited number of words. You can learn to plan and write a story that will make your readers look for more.

Here are some of the things you'll learn in *Quickies: Writing Short Fiction for the Romance Market:*

The History of the Short Story – Gain an understanding of the tradition of short stories and the difference between early stories and those written today.

Understanding Your Niche – Strategize how to work with the current market trends and the romance genre, the subgenres and the mash-ups that appeal to today's romance readers.

The Craft of Writing Short Romance – Learn the basics of storytelling, including setting, point of view, dialogue and characterization. Acquire insights to avoid some of the common pitfalls and give more in fewer words.

Use Writing Exercises – Practice developing a plot that will fit within your desired word length.

Layering – Add depth to your character and story.

Precision Writing – Develop techniques to select the correct words.

Note – This book is intended for authors with some experience in writing, who already understand the basics discussed briefly in the basics section.

DEDICATION

Thank you to all my family who put up with my constant reading and typing. I know I rarely look up from the keyboard, but when I do it is to see you. Thanks also to my friends in the Romance Writers of America and my local branch – the Romance Writers of Atlantic Canada.

Your support over the years has been invaluable.

TABLE OF CONTENTS

INTRODUCTION: So You Want to Write a Quickie

PART ONE: A BRIEF HISTORY OF SHORT FICTION – THEN AND NOW... 1

PART TWO: UNDERSTANDING YOUR NICHE – KNOW YOUR GENRE ... 7
- What Makes Romance?
- The Subgenres of Romance
- Mash-ups
- Writing for Different Age Groups
- Story Length – Categories

PART THREE: THE CRAFT OF WRITING SHORT ROMANCE ... 19
- A. The Basics
  - Structure of the Short Story
  - Point of View, 1st, 2nd, and 3rd Person, and Tense
  - Setting
  - Dialogue
  - Character Growth
  - Pacing

B. Archetypes, Themes, Tropes and Memes

C. The Short Plot Method
- Introductions
- Complications
- Climaxes
- Resolutions

Writing Exercise A . . . 45

PART FOUR: LAYERING . . . 47
- Adding Emotion
- Symbolism and Memes; The Rule of Three

Writing Exercise B . . . 52

PART FIVE: PRECISION WRITING . . . 55
- Keep it Concise – Avoid the Clichéd

Writing Exercise C . . . 56

PART SIX: KNOW YOUR MARKET . . . 61
- Who Reads Romance?
- Who Reads Short Romance Stories – Serials, Novellas, Shorts, and Anthologies?

PART SEVEN: CONCLUSION . . . 65

MORE ABOUT THE RED PEN COACH . . . 67

APPENDIX A: Further Suggested Reading . . . 69

APPENDIX B: Example of The Short Plot Method and Blank Form . . . 71

APPENDIX C: Current Short Fiction Opportunities, and Where to Look for Them . . . 76

INDEX . . . 81

ABOUT THE AUTHOR . . . 87

INTRODUCTION

So, you want to write a quickie – a short story or novella. Should be easy, right? A lot easier that writing a full length novel, yes?

No. Not really. All writing is more difficult than it appears to the reader, and writing a full story using a limited word count can be more than challenging.

Writing prose in a terse manner – getting everything across: beginning, middle, end, story arc and all – takes creativity, skill, and practice. The bonus is, once you've learned these strategies you can apply them to writing your full-length novels.

One question to ask yourself is this: Why do you want to write a short story, serial, or novella? Are you following what's known as a market trend? Or perhaps you simply think you should create a short piece to make your longer, related works more marketable. Is it because you believe you can make more money by producing more works more works more quickly? All of these might prove true if you have the discipline required to carry through.

There are other reasons to consider writing short fiction. It can be a great way to experiment with technique, perhaps allowing you to work within a different point of view or tense, or subject – a new genre, a philosophical thought, or political view. Shorter works can also provide a change of pace, a cleansing of the palate for a writer; they can inspire and they can teach. What better way to learn to convey an emotion or character or action than to really focus on using just the right words – taking the time to find the few that work so well there is no chance to mistake the meaning?

More than this, in today's market authors are encouraged to complete multiple releases each year to maintain and build the interest of their reading demographic. That pace is difficult to maintain if you stick to 80,000-plus word books. Novellas, published between longer works, can be a way to keep your name in the market and placing your short works in anthologies allows you to work with, and be presented alongside authors who have a slightly different market reach than you, increasing your chances for cross promotion and expanding your readership.

Finally, there is an intrinsic marketing opportunity in offering readers the "perma-free" short story. The cost of the time invested in writing your free offerings, the cost of editing, formatting and cover expenses, can become a smart marketing investment.

Many authors have chosen this route to promote a series, offering what might once have been a prologue or an epilogue, or perhaps an exploration of a secondary character as a bonus to the reader. It is hoped these shorts will pique readers' interest and – once familiar with the author's style and series characters – they will go out and buy the series.

In romance we have a varied and voracious audience. Readers constantly search for the next story and *demand* them from authors they enjoy. So short fiction makes sense for all of the above reasons and more. Offering shorts provides a way to keep readers happy and hooked and wanting to invest in the author.

PART ONE: A BRIEF HISTORY OF SHORT FICTION – THEN AND NOW

Few people who have passed through the school system today are unfamiliar with the structure of the short story. First marketed in the early 1800s, the short story evolved from the oral storytelling tradition where stories were told to educate about danger, provide epithets, and to share brief sections of epics. The stories were, for the most part, gothic in tone – for example, *The Tell-Tale Heart* by Edgar Allen Poe; *Rip Van Winkle*, by Washington Irving; and *Fairytales* by the Brothers Grimm.

The break from these traditions that led short fiction forward in its evolution was the development of the "gift book," a popular collection of poems, prose, and art given to upper class ladies. These trendy presents were the reason Nathaniel Hawthorne wrote the popular *Twice-Told Tales*, now a literary classic.

In the latter half of the 19th century and the first half of the 20th, short fiction morphed again and appeared in serialized stories printed in newspapers and journals. A number of authors took up the reins and the nature of the short stories varied from general fiction to detective stories, to romance and science fiction. Short story work sold well at that time and was so popular many of our iconic authors – F. Scott Fitzgerald, Ernest Hemmingway, and William Faulkner to name a few – turned to writing serials in order to pay their bills.

The peak of short fiction's popularity arrived after WWI. Basic reading literacy was nearly universal across North America and Europe, and "pulp" magazine sales boomed. At this point we saw the most experimentation within the stories, and successful authors of short fiction became too numerous to list. Writers played with genre, point of view, tense, and style, as well as incorporating edgy political and social commentary – including feminism and racial equality. These elements became factors and forces behind the short works of that time and perhaps nudged social change.

But nothing lasts forever. Technology evolved and the television arrived. Catalyzing a near-death experience for short fiction in general, TV viewing took over reading time and suffused our entertainment desires. Pulp magazine sales dwindled and most magazine publishers closed. The novella, the serial, and the short story nearly disappeared as a consequence. In 2007, **Stephen King**[1] wrote an article for *The New York Times Book Review* talking about the state of the short story. He stated: *"The American short story is alive and well,"* and went on to pose this question, *"Do you like the sound of that?"* Then he flippantly answered with, *"Me too. I only wish it were actually true."*

Shortly after this article was published the first e-reader appeared on the market. Technology became the short-story author's friend, as the printing press had been more than a century earlier. Today, the Internet flourishes along with e-books. In our fast-paced society, the amount of time a reader spends reading at one sitting, is often limited…and so the short story, the novella, and the serial, have wide appeal once again.

---

[1] Stephen King – award winning author of short fiction and horror, learn more about him here: **http://stephenking.com/**

Neil Gaiman[2] writes this about the short story:

"Like some kind of particularly tenacious vampire, the short story refuses to die, and seems at this point in time to be a wonderful length for our generation."

People read on the bus or the train on their way to work. They consume fiction on their iPads and their cell phones and their e-readers. Certainly, Edgar Allen Poe's belief that the short story was a tale that could be read in one sitting is as apt now as it was then.

There is a vast market for short fiction. Online magazines – e-zines and blogs – often include short stories and serials; and anthologies, boxed sets and e-publishers are calling for, and accepting more and more novellas. Even the short-short story's appeal (once the common fable or anecdote, and later used by authors such as Leo Tolstoy, James Joyce and Ernest Hemmingway, short fiction can be anywhere from one paragraph to 2500 words) has returned under the moniker of flash fiction.

---

[2] Neil Gaiman - award winning author of short fiction. Learn more about him and his work here: **http://www.neilgaiman.com/**

The renaissance of short fiction is now and the opportunity to sell short fiction is real.

6   NANCY CASSIDY

PART TWO: UNDERSTANDING YOUR NICHE

What Makes Romance?

How does knowing your genre help the modern romance writer and reader? **Romance Writers of America**, the largest non-profit trade association of Romance Writers in North America, describes romance this way:

"Two basic elements comprise every romance novel: a central love story and an emotionally satisfying and optimistic ending.

"A Central Love Story: The main plot centers around individuals falling in love and struggling to make the relationship work. A writer can include as many subplots as he/she wants as long as the love story is the main focus of the novel.

"An Emotionally Satisfying and Optimistic Ending: In a romance, the lovers who risk and struggle for each other and their relationship are rewarded with emotional justice and unconditional love.

8   NANCY CASSIDY

"Romance novels may have any tone or style, be set in any place or time, and have varying levels of sensuality – ranging from sweet to extremely hot. These settings and distinctions of plot create specific subgenres within romance fiction." [3]

RWA's definition covers the basics of the genre, but nothing stays static in the publishing world. Happy Ever After (HEA), as referred to above as the emotionally satisfying and optimistic ending, has expanded to allow Happy For Now (HFN), a less permanent situation that remains upbeat but doesn't imply that there is nowhere for the main character to go beyond marriage once the story ends. The key remains that at the end of the story the reader is satisfied – they leave the story with a smile on their face.

---

[3] Romance Writers of America Organization, Romance Genre, About the Romance Genre Web. 5 Jan. 2015.
http://www.rwa.org/p/cm/ld/fid=578

The Subgenres of Romance

There is no exhaustive list of romance subgenres. In truth, there is an ever-evolving series of categorizations that are monitored by no one, yet followed by the readers almost before the authors of romance recognize the changes. But, some of the most common larger subgenres – categorization based on level of heat (sexual) in the relationships featured in the stories, time period, character age and fantastic nature of the story – are as follows:

Historical Romance – Any book based on a time period more than 50 years in the past. Most common are the Regency, Victorian, Medieval, Western, and early 1900s romances (often referred to as Flapper or Wartime romances). Historical romances feature activities, fashion, and can include religious and political viewpoints of the time.

Historical romance can be further divided and defined by location, with many books set in England for older eras, or the United States for the more modern ones. There is also another small category devoted to historical romances set in other countries with non-English civilizations, i.e. Egyptian, Mayan, and Australian.

Contemporary Romance – Set in modern times, these romances tend to focus on the relationship between the main characters rather than an external plot. The story revolves around character development and relationship development, sometimes highlighted with elements such as humor or mystery.

Paranormal Romance – In this subgenre, fantasy and gothic elements are paired with romance, bringing in such things as magic, the fae, werewolves, vampires, and ghosts. These are usually set in modern times but must include world building that sets the world of the story apart from the kind of real modern life presented in contemporary books.

Science Fiction Romance – Although usually set in the future, this subgenre has much in common with the paranormal subgenre of romance in that the reader must experience a suspension of belief. These stories are usually set in the future; may include fantastical elements such as aliens and other world settings; and are reliant on the author's ability to build a reality that is different, but not too different than the reader is familiar with.

Romantic Suspense – The external suspense plot in this kind of story must be equally strong and follow alongside the development of the relationship between the main characters. The romantic suspense story must also place those characters in a dangerous environment, and they must attempt to extract themselves from it while solving some mystery. This can be expressed casually, in a problem-solving manner, which would be considered a *cozy mystery*; or at a higher-stakes level, considered *suspense/mystery*; or at a constant level of life-threatening danger in the *thriller*.

Inspirational or Christian Romance – Religious or moral societal beliefs are an integral part of the life and character development of the main characters in these stories. It can play a large part in the relationship development or present obstacles to the development of the romance.

Young Adult/New Adult Romance – This subgenre presents characters of a certain age and the common issues they tend to face. For young adults aged 16–19, these issues might include the problems and pressures faced in high school; the new experiences – driving, drinking, love and sexual activities; and the new responsibilities – first job, sibling care, school marks, etc. For new adults, aged 19–22, it's University life; more varied sexual experiences; greater responsibilities – first career, marriage, parenthood.

Erotic Romance – This genre is based on high sexual level alone. Erotic romance novels can incorporate elements of any of the other subgenres, but the development of the sexual relationship is the core of the story. There must be a reason for the high sexuality level and the progress of it, or the stories would not be considered romance.

Mash-Ups: Mix 'em Up

Mash-ups are the deliberate combination of two or more subgenres. Mash-ups can be created in two ways. The first is to create a crossover using combinations of the subgenres of romance – erotic paranormal romances, romantic thrillers in space, inspirational romance in eras past. How about a Christian romantic suspense? For an example, review award-winning *Firelight* by Kristen Callihan.[4] Her books represent one form of mash-up meshing the subgenres of erotic, paranormal, and historic. The second, currently popular mash-up technique is to take a well-known story classic, and blend it with a new situation – for example *Pride and Prejudice and Zombies* by Seth Grahame- Smith.[5] This second

---

[4] Firelight by Kristen Callihan http://www.amazon.com/Firelight-Darkest-London-Book-1-ebook/dp/B0052AI09Q

[5] Pride and Prejudice and Zombies by Seth Grahame-Smith http://www.goodreads.com/book/show/5899779-pride-and-prejudice-and-zombies

approach has been lucrative for certain authors, but this kind of adaptation of a successful story plot is considered a fad, and the appeal of this kind of short story is not expected to last long. As always, what works in romance for the long run is creating sympathy for characters and the evocation of real emotion, no matter how unreal the situation.

Writing for Different Age Groups

As mentioned above, there are two subgenres that demand specific age requirements for the main characters. What cannot be misunderstood though, is that your reader may not – in fact, will probably not – be of the age group referenced in your story. Young Adult and New Adult, while certainly selling to those age groups, sell even more frequently to older readers.

So what must be considered when writing stories in these two genres?

Language for one thing: Writers need to stay current with idiom and speech patterns used by this age group. Authors of these subgenres are not likely to be young adults themselves, they must be familiar with the language and lifestyles of young adults in order to portray them with accuracy. This does not mean that dialogue should be overburdened with trending slang, but it is important not to use expressions that are ten years out of date. Another consideration is not to date your work with something briefly popular (i.e. referencing a pop star, a current scandal) that may be considered inconsequential or irrelevant by readers in a few years. There is a delicate balance to aim for.

Writers must stretch back and reach for that sense of newness and energy and angst that permeates this stage of life and that of new adults. They must write in the fear, the hormones, the fun. Even more importantly, the author must not "write down" to the readers' assumed age. Teens and young adults of today are intelligent, and far more worldly than older authors attempting the genre might assume. Writers must understand that their own personal naivety means they must observe and research to understand and present what is happening to a character or the ramifications of a new situation.

Story Length Categories

There are so many words to qualify current fiction: novel, epic, novella, short story, short-short, flash, serial fiction, and the anthology-length story. There are others, but basically stories can be categorized into five lengths that publishers and readers are looking for:

Epic or longer novel: This range varies slightly (as they all do) but is generally considered to be works from 80,000 to 110,000 words. While there are books that are longer, there aren't many.

Novel: The novel is considered to be 40,000 to 79,999 words. This length is most popular with e-publishers and publishers looking for works that will be published in paper as well as electronically.

Novella: The novella's word count is generally 15,000 to 39,999. Most publishers consider anything under 40,000 words to be a novella. You often see novella collections in indie-published boxed sets.

Sub-Category – Serial: The Serial is created when a much longer story is broken down into novella-length sections, ranging from 15,000 to 25,000 words. The sections are often released fairly quickly (every two to four weeks), one after the other, and are meant to be read in order, not as stand-alone material.

Anthology length, Novelette or Short Novella: Works in these categories range in length from 3,000 to 14,999 words. Most publishers, or groups of authors publishing together, want to fit a good number of authors into an anthology without going over a 300-page limit for print. While some will work with longer novellas (and thus fewer authors) this is not the norm. You may see this length in boxed sets as well – simply a newer form of anthology that digital-only publishing allows. It downloads without the worry or confines of page length and some contain collections of full novel-length books packaged together.

Short Story, Short-short, or Flash Fiction: These works are under 3,000 words in length. Some publishers allow more. This length is most common for magazines, anthologies, online "perma-free" – permanently free stories offered by authors to promote a series. These can go as high as 8,000 words for blog posts and entry in some competitions.

Part Three: The Craft of Writing Short Romance

The Basics

It is important to note that this book has been written with the idea that the reader and potential short-story author has some experience in writing and a good grasp of writing techniques – these basic elements are important tools in all writing and have less to do with what makes a short story short than what makes any writing good and easy to read. If anything mentioned here is unfamiliar, the writer should check the list of recommended reading in Appendix A.

Abby Weeks[6]**,** says this of writing serials:

"They allow me to get into a story and blow it up into an exciting situation very quickly. Most of my serials are around 20,000 words in length, and I find that writing in this format forces me to build up to some sort of climax by the end ofthe first installment. If I was writing a

---

[6] Abby Weeks is a popular author who gained a large following by writing serials. Find out more about her here: **http://www.amazon.com/Abby-Weeks/e/B00FAP1SR4**

novel, I would be forced to structure the story differently..."

Structure of the Short Story

So now that you have decided to write a romance short story, and you know what genre and subgenre it is, what makes writing a short story – or novella – any different than writing a novel? Beyond length, what is there about a short story that makes it a separate category of fiction?

The major difference is in the construction of the story arc, the chronological construction of the plot. There are two story arcs in most romance novels – the external action arc, and the romantic arc. Usually, in the case of longer romantic fiction, these two arcs follow each other and follow a pattern that is like a long, smooth series of sine waves, as below.

The story tends to begin on an upswing where everything is going great until there is a plot twist and the momentum takes the plot and characters in a downward swing. Each twist creates a crest or a trough in the story in terms of level of difficulty for the characters to proceed through the events – together.

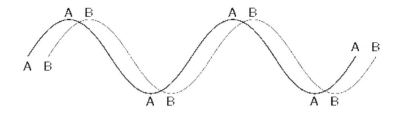

Stories can also begin on a downswing where the characters are thrown together in the midst of everything going wrong. In romance the story always ends on the upswing – leading to the HEA or HFN – no matter how it begins.

The romantic arc can often be portrayed as a matching wave line where the characters' emotions respond to the twists and turns of the external plot. The emotional low before the final crest (happy ending) is often termed the "black moment" – when all seems lost and it's unlikely the romance will work out.

In short fiction, the overall story arc looks more like a heartbeat with sharp turns, steep drops.

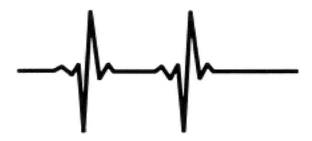

There are usually fewer of these because everything is compressed due to restricted word count. Some stories are so short they encapsulate only one scene, so the twists are more extreme and the time they cover can be quite brief. Action must be completed quickly, and attraction and love acquired at a fast pace. For this reason many authors make use of memes, themes and tropes – generalized ideas that readers of the genre recognize and have some expectations about – more on these shortly. Authors also use a few handy shortcuts, including giving the main characters a previous relationship, using archetypal characters (at least on the surface), and keeping everything in one location.

Alternatively, in some short stories, the arc can be as simple as a single, sweeping curve.

Because these stories have a small word count and cover a small amount of time, the main characters' relationship development is smoother, with fewer dips and crests, even to the point of having none of these. In that case, the story is all about the event that causes the characters' relationship to change. There may, in fact, be no black moment – the point in which the romance seems doomed to fail, usually occurring in the last quarter of the story – at all, which some authors are shocked to discover. For those stories, the black moment simply isn't necessary and there isn't time to have it unfold.

Point of View, 1st Person, 2nd Person, 3rd Person, and Tense

The point of view (POV) refers to the viewpoint from which a story is told. There are a few important POV questions to address when developing a story for short fiction:

- Whose story should it be?

- How can you show what it is the character sees, hears, feels, tastes, smells, experiences?

- How can you show what characters are experiencing emotionally without coming right out and saying it?

Quite often, in a short piece, there is really only time to tell the story from one POV. We don't have the word count to explore a scene from two or more viewpoints as can be done in longer romantic fiction. So the crucial question becomes whose story is it? Who experiences the greatest character growth within the confines of the story? The answers to these questions provides the best POV from which to approach the story.

In longer pieces of short fiction (novellas, serials) two viewpoints are often entertained, usually those of the main couple featured in the romantic arc of the story. It is recommended that use of additional viewpoints (the villain, secondary characters) be curtailed so there is greater opportunity to delve into the viewpoints of the romance's couple. If there are more than two people in the romance, a third viewpoint may be included, but more than that simply becomes confusing for the short-story reader.

1st, 2nd, and 3rd person refer to consistent use of specific pronouns to represent the point of view used to narrate a story.

First person POV uses the pronouns I, we, me, us, my, mine. An example of a first person POV would be a sentence like this:

I ran across the street because we had a meeting in five minutes.

Telling a story from the 1st person point of view was once left to writers of autobiographies, but use of first person POV has become popular in young adult fiction, urban fantasy, and some romance. In most stories using first person POV we only see one character's POV, allowing the reader to settle deep into the mindset of the character, and avoiding confusion caused by having more than one character addressing themselves as I.

Second person POV uses the pronouns you, your, yours. This isn't easily used in fiction, although it does appear in middle-grade choose-your-own-adventure or gaming fiction. Here's an example:

You run across the street because you have a meeting in five minutes.

Third person POV uses the pronouns she, he, it, they, his, hers, its, theirs, him, her, them. This is the most common POV used in fiction. It allows for more point of views to be comfortably understood, since there is some separation between reader and character. But when 'they' is used as the main pronoun – rather than he or she – it is often presented in an omnipresent way, as if the narrator knows everything that every character is doing and feeling at all points of time. This causes greater distance between reader and character and is generally disliked by readers. They cannot connect with the characters in the same way as they do reading stories written with 'he' or 'she' as the main pronoun. Likewise, having too many POVs can be confusing and doesn't allow enough time with each to establish a degree of caring from the reader for each character.

Tense must also be considered for your POV. The verb tense tells when the action takes place. Past and present tense are used commonly in romance, with past tense being the most common and present tense sometimes being linked with 1st person POV. Future tense is not generally considered for extended use in genre fiction. Here are examples of each tense in the simple format:

Past: *She jumped at the strange sound.*
Present: *She jumps at the strange sound.*
Future: *She will jump at the strange sound.*

Each tense has a simple form (jump, jumped, will jump), progressive (is jumping, was jumping, will be jumping), perfect (has jumped, had jumped, will have jumped), and progressive perfect form (has been jumping, had been jumping, will have been jumping). As needed the verbs can change into the various forms of each tense. Simple form is the most regularly used form and it keeps the action moving without added formality and word count.

Choose your POV wisely.

Setting

Although setting remains crucial to any storytelling, typically, the shorter the story, the fewer details we have time to disclose. For this reason the shortest stories often remain in one location, and description includes elements of atmosphere and implication as much as physical detail. For instance, use of the weather, while somewhat cliché, remains a strong tool in setting the atmosphere – gloomy weather, gloomy character/situation. Details in the setting can also reveal the passage of time – sunrise, sunset, high noon, the seasons. It is important to remember that setting is not ignored in short fiction. Even in the shortest short, setting is a crucial element along with character and plot. In order to save time, or word count, setting can be slipped into the narration without a large amount of detail. For instance the sound of waves and gulls can indicate the beach; a character wearing a hat and scarf can reveal the season.

Dialogue

Dialogue can be divided into categories—the verbal and the non-verbal, sometimes referred to as internal.

Dialogue can be used to provide information as shown in this sentence:

"Hi, my name is Anne. I saw you sitting here alone. You look sad, are you OK?"

But it is often better to use narrative to show what is happening and use verbal dialogue to move a scene forward, initiate action, and give insight into characters, as in this sentence:

Anne spotted the boy on the curb, his small face wet with tears. She straightened her shoulders and walked to her newest charge. "Hi, are you OK?"

While you might think that this adds unnecessary words to a shorter work, this method is often used for writing longer novels or shorter pieces. It pays, in the long run, to keep verbal dialogue moving and reveal more with narrative.

A second issue with verbal dialogue is the dreaded speech tag – he said, she said. You will notice in the above examples there are no tags. Quite often they are simply not needed when proper narrative reveals the identity of the speaker. If they are needed, it is helpful to keep the tags very simple: "he said" rather than "he whined loudly." The dialogue and narrative text accompanying it should describe the way the character is speaking. Taking a shortcut—cutting the word count by cutting the detail—with a speech tag, does not pay.

Non-verbal dialogue, or internal thought, is often expressed in italics and put in present tense. For example:

Anne held his hand. *Here we go again.*

While internal thought can be very helpful in areas where narration can overload the word count, internal dialogue can easily be overused – especially if the writer gets a little lazy.

On another note, some publishers have opted not to have internal thought in italics unless the character is literally speaking to themselves. Instead, they ask that the thought be built into the narrative and not necessarily written in the present tense. See the example below:

Anne shrugged. *I can't help it if he can't answer the question.*

vs.

Anne shrugged. She couldn't help it if he couldn't answer the question.

Character Growth

Characters should change throughout the course of a story. When writing a book, aim to have both static and dynamic characters. Dynamic characters are the main characters – in romance, the romantic couple – and they change and develop throughout the book. Both experience growth by passing over and through and around the obstacles and challenges presented to them, or their relationship.

Static characters, on the other hand, are those in the story who do not change – they do not noticeably learn, change, or grow, and are not meant to. They are not the focus of the story but are there to provide setting, comic relief, information, or impetus to the story. For example, a static character could be in the story for a short period and die in such a way their death could become the impetus for the growth of a main character.

In traditional romance formats, both members of the couple will be dynamic, learning and growing through their changing relationship and the trials they face singly, or together.

It is important for the author to understand and reveal something to the reader about why a character acts a given way. Their history and background, the events that motivate them must be known and understood completely by the author, but might not be totally revealed to the reader. Certainly not at the beginning of the story for the reader, and perhaps not in their entirety even by the end, but without this knowledge, the author will not be able to ensure that their characters continue to act and react in a way that is true to who they are.

In romance, how your characters change is the heart of the story. We ask what will each character sacrifice for the other?

Each character must also have motivations – things that drives them forward in their actions. These can be both internal and external and often are not the same as their goals, meaning what the character believes they want. Conflict is created when there are differences between motivations and goals, meaning what the character wants and what they really need in order to be fulfilled, are often at odds with each other.[7]

In a short story there may not be enough time to have both main characters in a relationship change, or for the changes to be on a grand scale. Often, if you do try to press this level of change into a short time period, the results aren't

---

[7] For more on this and the GMC concept, read Goal, Motivation and Conflict by Debra Dixon, as listed in Appendix B for suggested further reading.

believable. But at least one character must grow in order for a romance to be possible. Perhaps it is only growth in that they find a way to make room in their lives or hearts for another, which can represent a bigger change than you imagine.

Pacing

As mentioned previously in the discussion of the story arc for a short story, the twists and turns that create the pace of short fiction happen quickly. There may be a number of short, quick twists in externally motivated plots, and fewer in internally motivated plots, but the pace at which change occurs is always rapid. There is no time for scenes around a dinner table, with characters discussing the day's events or describing the food. Such scenes drag a short story down, slow the pace, and may unbalance the story. Each scene must push the story forward.

If you follow the scene-and-sequel method of pacing[8], where each scene dictates the action

---

[8] For more on the scene and sequel method, read *Elements of Fiction Writing – Scene & Structure* by Jack Bickham
http://www.amazon.com/gp/product/B00D0AH01E

and the sequel reveals the reaction of the characters to the action – in other words the cause and effect of each plot twist – you may find the smooth pacing of a short story to be both easier and more difficult to achieve. Meaning, there is little time for reaction, yet the effect of the action or twist must be clearly felt by the characters and conveyed to the reader. It is not always necessary to show reactions to every action.

Scenes are necessary to reveal the peaks or troughs in the story arc and to move the plot forward.

The pace of the scene can be speeded up using short sentences filled with action. A short sentence reads faster. Another method is to insert dialogue in narration. Avoid using this too often as too much dialogue can dull the progress of the scene, but used in a balanced way, dialogue can cut word count.

Alternative ways to change the pace include foreshadowing or flashbacks. In the case of the flashback, often written as another scene, the flashback can create a comparison with a scene from the present where readers will draw their own conclusions. In foreshadowing, pace of the short fiction can be kept brisk by asking a question, or opening narrative with an out-of place-detail, the purpose of which will become obvious in a later scene.

Em Petrova[9] advises this when writing novellas:

"Have a strong GMC for hero and heroine but streamline so you're not trying to cram an 80k word plot into 20k words. Come late to the party and leave early—start in the middle of the action and leave just shy of the reader wanting the book to end."

Archetypes, Themes, Tropes, and Memes

What are archetypes, themes, tropes, and memes? What is the difference between them?

---

[9] Em Petrova is a popular author of erotic romance. Find out more about her here: **http://www.empetrova.com/**

For the purpose of this book, archetypes can be considered generalizations about a character. Here are several examples of the two-word descriptions comprised of an internal reality and an external "face":

1. the lonely cowboy
2. the tortured (regretful) fireman
3. the alpha leader (think CEO)
4. the sensitive tough guy
5. the sexy professor
6. the sexy tough girl (female cop, etc.)
7. the secretive survivor (she lived through it and
8. doesn't want to share)
9. the naïve go-getter

There are many more of these, but by simplifying the description of the character to these two elements we can identify a conflict arising from the two words.

In romance, **theme** is the underlying message of the story. It's what a reader takes away when they finish reading. It can be something as simple as the uplifting joy of falling love. This could be the theme of a lighthearted or sweet romance story. Or perhaps you want to convey the process of separation and reunion – second chances. Or the healing power of love where characters must overcome serious internal issues. Themes in romance are positive and optimistic, due for the most part, to the tradition of the happy-ever-after ending.

Tropes are recurring plot patterns. Readers can recognize these and from them they understand what they can expect from a story.

According to Romance Writers of America[10] the following are the "Top 10 popular romance tropes":

(1) friends to lovers;
(2) soul mate/fate;
(3) second chance at love;
(4) secret romance;
(5) first love;
(6) strong hero/heroine;
(7) reunited lovers;
(8) love triangle;
(9) sexy billionaire/millionaire;
(10) sassy heroine

---

[10] Romance Writers of America: The Romance Genre: **https://www.rwa.org/p/cm/ld/fid=582**

A **meme** is an unspoken but generally accepted and understood description. For instance, in science fiction, mentioning a scene occurs in the warp drive engineering room implies certain things – unspoken is the fact they are on a spaceship capable of traveling through the galaxy; in young adult literature, referencing the high school gym implies a large open space, with high ceilings, a sweaty smell, and a mild feeling of terror, for those who hated those classes. In romance there are many accepted memes such as the concept of the fated mate, the importance of the first dance. Memes are innately understood by regular readers of the genre, and one of the key reasons writers of the genre – romance writers – should be readers of romance. To fully grasp the subtleties, it is prudent for writers of short romance to be reading popular short romance.

Jasinda Wilder[11] says this about Writing Short :

> *In short stories or novellas, every word counts. Every paragraph has to be focused and sharpened. You have to develop your characters quickly, set out your plot within*

---

[11] Jasinda Wilder is a popular author of contemporary series romance. Find out more about her here: **http://jasindawilder.com/**

moments and use every scene and word of dialogue to push it to conclusion. It's kind of like a shot of espresso versus a big mug of coffee..."

The Short Plot Method

Plotting your short story may seem like an unnecessary evil, but it could save you time. There are some ways to keep the plot simple, and in this book we will use my Short Plot Method that focuses on introductions, complications, climaxes, and resolutions.

Introductions

The shorter the story, the less room there is for multiple characters and secondary plots. The shorter the story, the closer you are to the conclusion, even at the beginning. Your introduction needs to be concise and engaging. . .

But not that short!

As previously stated, short stories might only contain one or two characters. A novella might have three or four. In a novel-length work a writer can expand on numbers and include an entire lifetime of connections.

A short story usually focuses on a single event. There is no room for anything unnecessary. A novella is a bit of a combination of the novel and the short story – there is still no room for lack of cohesiveness. It must focus on a few people and a few events, and has only limited space to explore the elements of the story.

Using The Short Plot Method, the author begins by creating a scenario where the characters already know each other, or of each other, and can make some assumptions about each other. The author introduces the action and the characters to the reader rather than to each other. An already established relationship of some sort allows the author to build on the growth of that relationship. This does not mean that your characters had to have a romantic interaction previously. It does mean they have met before. Perhaps they are friends, or rivals, or friends of friends, or an older brother's best friend, etc. Or perhaps they really were in a relationship before, or still are, but are looking for renewal.

This brings us to the characters themselves and our use of archetypes. Using the two-word archetype during plotting – discussed in the previous pages – allows the author to have a grasp of the character's personality and issues, but it is the use of trope – the recognizable plot pattern – that really makes the issues stand out and clarifies motivations of the characters.

Common tropes include these: accidental pregnancy, boss/employee, friends to lovers, enemies to lovers, amnesia, one-night stand, matchmaker, reunited lovers, billionaire playboy, love triangle, different worlds, older brother's best friend, ugly duckling, fish out of water, falling for savior, and marriage of convenience.

Don't forget your subgenre – if it is paranormal romance, for instance, the story requires certain world building efforts; if historic, thought has to be put into the roles of the characters of the time, etc. At this point genre memes are helpful to keep the word count down while still getting the theme of the story across.

Each main character will have a goal based on their two-word archetype – something they really want. It may or may not be what they actually need. This desire is what initially motivates the character and may change in a longer novella, but likely remains the main desire in a shorter story. To keep things simple, the goal or want may be directly linked to a need. With care, goals and wants can be set up to conflict with one other.

Example: *In a the case of a story of older brother's best friend, the goal of the girl is to finally get her brother's best friend to recognize her as an attractive woman and desire her. The goal of the boy may be to resist his attraction to the girl based on an old promise to his friend, the girl's brother, to protect the girl.*

Complications

As we discussed earlier, a short story has turning points like a novel, but there are fewer of them. Beyond the introduction to the characters and setting, there is an initiating action, growing action, and a climax, followed by a conclusion and resolution in both.

Complications do not mean the addition of more conflict to the initial conflict set up early on. Complications are the twist-of-the-knife events that tweak or twist the main conflict into a greater level of difficulty. In our example used above, the complication could be that the two are forced to spend more time together in an intimate or close-quarter situation.

Climaxes

There may actually be more than one climax in the plot, depending on the length of your story—novella vs. short story—but yes, we are already there! How many climaxes there are depends on how many complications you have introduced; each obstacle the characters overcome adds a kind of climax to the relationship.

Each climax has major impact on the relationship, and if you have time for the anticlimax or black moment before the final triumph, that too must have major impact.

Resolutions

Because we are writing romance, we do need a happy ever after, or at least a happy for now ending. It's one of the very few rules that applies to all romance genres. While everything else about romance has changed over the years, whether you are writing about a sweet romance, a couple of cowboys, or a vampire threesome, your reader expects that smile at the end of the story.

Writing Exercise A:

Please See Appendix B for an example of my Short Plot Method in use, and for a blank form for you to try. To have both forms on hand during the next section will clarify some points.

1. Label the form with your genre/subgenre and estimated story length. Decide where this story takes place and over what time period (setting). Keep in mind that any change of location takes up valuable word count.

2. Write a one-liner that introduces the characters and their relationship to each other. Use two archetypes – page 37, and use a trope, – page 38 – that describe an existing relationship. Label each character's conflicting internal goal.

3. Write one line about the inciting incident – the event that makes the characters' relationship change.

4. Write one line about the complication. For a longer story, write a second line about the issue, and what happens that creates a change in the relationship.

5. Write one line on the climax, and a second one if you have a second peak in your curve, and a third line if there is an anticlimax. Remember, in shorter works, 15,000 and under, you may not have a black moment or anticlimax.

6. Give a one-line happy ending and you're ready to write your piece of short fiction.

Part Four: Layering

On first glance, your simple plot outline will seem *too* simple and even...even clichéd. Of course it is! This is only your mini-plot outlining what's going to happen in the simplest of terms. Now we layer in character depth, symbolism, allusion, and description. These take the story from cliché to a story with depth. But the process you went through for Exercise A illustrates a minimum of plot that can actually comprise a short story.

*Note – *Often authors try to fit too much plot into a small word count, and don't leave time or words for layering.*

Adding Emotion

This is the part that makes the story something that the reader will not forget – character depth and emotional connection to the reader. It's the part of the book that clings to readers emotionally, even after the last page is read. Authors who do this well, write the books with heroes we love and heroines we dream of being. There appear to be two ways to inspire emotional connection in readers:

With strong writing:

1. Word Choices and Active vs. Passive Sentences: Get rid of those state-of-being, those "was" and "were" passages. There is almost always a better verb and form to use. And when considering verbs, get rid of weak verbs – often the "ing" verb forms. Use verbs and use verb forms that give a stronger emotional punch and a sense of immediacy. In active writing the subject of the sentence usually comes first, as it performs the action. For example:

Passive – *Her mood was destroyed by his careless action.*
Active – *His careless action destroyed her mood.*

Passive – *The lamb was bitten by the lion.*
Active – *The lion bit the lamb.* (or attacked, eviscerated, shredded – go for the most powerful word choice! See more on this in Part Five)

2. Writing that engages all five senses. Many authors forget this and stick to using sight descriptors only. What about

smell? Taste? Touch? Sound? Yes, this adds word count, but using different senses can be worth it. A single evocative image can ground the scene and prevent the need for repeated descriptions later.

- Sight – *She looked like an angel, dressed in white.*
- Sight and touch – *The layers of her dress glowed in different shades of white and as she walked he heard the muted sway of the chiffon, like angels' feathers.*
- Scent and touch – *He caught the scent of lavender as she rushed by, the layers of her skirts sending a breath of air through the stale ballroom like the brush of wings against his skin.*

3.   It's not always about the character; these senses can help create a mood that influences the emotion of the character and how the reader interprets their actions. For example:

4.

The dark clouds sent shadows across her face. She'd made her decision.

vs.

The bright sunlight lit up her face. She'd made her decision.

5.   Body language – showing vs. telling a character's emotion – complements the POV of the character, and allows the reader to settle deeper into the character's mindset and emotions.

She hated him. He was the last person she'd agree to marry.

vs.

She clenched his gift in her hand, crushing the delicate silk. She glared at him and let the handkerchief fall to the ground. Let that be his answer.

Remove all the filter words – he thought, he felt, he imagined, he believed. This is especially important when writing in 1st person.

From within – inspiring yourself:

Try to remember when writing the emotion into your characters that for your readers to feel that emotion, you, as the author, must first feel it. If you weep, the reader weeps.

How does a writer inspire that kind of writing for themselves? Many authors use theme music to get in the mood or watch an inspiring scene or movie. Browsing pictures can also help. Storyboarding – the creation of a collage that represents your book or scene – is one method for creating a visual cue to inspire the writer to the emotion they intend to portray. Pictures don't always have to look like the character to embody the emotion or attitude of the character.

Knowing the character well is important, even in a short story, and even if all you know doesn't get written into the story, you must know them to understand why your character does what they do – their goals and motivations. This means being familiar with their backstory, physical description, name, friends and family, position in the world, and their nemeses. Then go further: Know their strengths and weaknesses, their skills and abilities. Their goals, motivation, and conflict can push the plot forward for you to follow. To write well, become familiar with their fears and understand their dialogue style, gestures, mannerisms, and quirks that can connect readers. It is important for you to know these things so characters can represent themselves at all times.

A great way to do this is to interview your character. Ask them all sorts of questions. Take the time to do this; it will be worth it. The more you know, the less you have to tell your readers. The details will edge into your writing without you actively choosing to insert them.

Writing Exercise B:

Conduct an interview with your character, however brief. Ask about his life before the story.

Strike a balance: strengths vs. weaknesses and needs referencing their internal strength. If a character is all good – good at every single thing, we will not love him or find him sympathetic. What flaw might make him seem more real and likeable?

Skills and Abilities – Every skill a person develops has come at a cost. This is true for your character – time, blood, sweat, or tears. What are his abilities and what have they cost him?

Think Superman and Kryptonite: Vulnerabilities must balance our character's powers. What are the character's vulnerabilities?

GMC: This is the concept including each major character's goal, their motivation, and their conflicts as the driving forces in the story – or at least in the changing of the character's developmental arc. See further recommended reading to find out more, but basically GMC integrates what your characters think they want, what they need, and what is stopping them from achieving their goals.

* * *

Symbolism and Memes; The Rule of Three

Another aspect of layering involves the story structure. As previously discussed, each subgenre of romance has its memes – the literary principles or events or descriptions that have been used or repeated throughout the genre so many times they are generally understood. These could include the idea of the fated mate in paranormal romance or the idea of a warp drive in science fiction – something yet to be invented, that could take humanity across the universe. Memes in romance include the usual stages in sexual relations development, like the first touch, the first kiss, or the first dance because these are pivotal and universal moments in romance.

Symbolism and memes can be used to help layer the plot. It is best to use these in a repetitive manner, about three times in the story. Less and the pattern isn't visible, more and it seems aggressive, as if you're not trusting the reader to understand.

Symbolism in stories usually represents a level of the trope being used in the plot. For example, if the trope is enemies to lovers, the symbol will represent the initial confrontation or conflict that led to the status of enemy. Divorce papers for instance. Because we must economize on words, it is essential that whenever something is shown, it is shown for a reason. And for something to be shown multiple times – the rule of three – the object/symbol must also have an impact on the character's development or growth, perhaps represent the way they change throughout the story.

It's also important to understand that a symbol can be anything: a dried rose, the front door of a house, or an empty diary. But if those symbols are to be associated with something that isn't immediately understood, the symbolic relationship must be made explicit, if not on first appearance, then on the second.

Part Five: Precision Writing

Keep it Concise – Avoid Clichéd

Because word count is crucial to short fiction construction, care in word choice is vital. The selection of words to convey the greatest meaning in the most concise way is important in any writing, but even more so in short fiction because without it, you simply run out of space.

This is something you can work on during self-edits. To be concise, three things are important:

- Be clear: Use active writing vs. passive. Say things simply.
- Be precise: Choose nouns that most accurately describe what you want to name.
- Be tight: Find words that multi-task. Use verbs that convey emotion as well as action.

Writing Exercise C:

How would you rewrite this sentence concisely without losing the intent? How few words can you use to do this?

The waiter pulled out her chair and she sat down at the candle-lit table and breathed a great sigh of relief; no matter how late she was, she was still there first.

Consider: She took her seat and heaved a sigh. Late, but still before him.

Some words have little to say in terms of emotional meaning. Others can convey a lot. These examples include verbs that lend themselves to terse, concise prose, yet offer more action and emotion. These verbs offer some insight about the enactor's emotional status while committing these actions. Here is a quick exercise on verb choice:

Give a more punchy alternative to each of these:

Example: *Walked – shuffled, bounced, strode, fled*

Moved

Closed

Breathed

Avoid any form of the verb "to be" – but that's a whole other topic (Active vs. Passive writing).

The precise selection of a just-right noun can save space and add to readers' understanding. Be as specific as possible.

Give a couple alternatives:

Example: *Male – boy, man, youth*

Flower

Party

* * *

Avoiding clichés:
Too often we see the same, tired scenes in romance. But in short romance, clichés can be rampant. The biggest cliché is insta-love or insta-lust. This is to be avoided at all cost. For example, a scene where the heroine looks across the room and instantly finds her heart is beating with desire or love as she gazes upon the hero for the first time. This kind of a fast-track to love is completely unbelievable. While attraction is often derived from appearance, there must be more to

create sexual tension and for desire to be believable. Fate alone, as the sole reason for two people to be together, is also a cliché to avoid. While lovers may be fated, believing and succumbing to that fate in the first chapter will have the reader abandoning the book in disbelief.

Here are some other clichés to avoid: where the hero or heroine describes themselves while looking in a mirror; the heavy use of adjectives when describing the heroine's appearance (or overuse of adjectives anywhere); all historical male figures being rakes who never want to marry; and the woman who is obviously beautiful yet doesn't believe herself to be beautiful.

Caution should be applied to love scenes, in particular. If hotter seems to be the trend in today's short fiction, why repeat the same tired sexual themes? Overused clichés can include the virgin heroine; first-time sex that is painless; panties that literally become sopping; forgetting to take precautions against pregnancy or sexually transmitted disease in modern romances; *only* the hero being able to satisfy the heroine, despite the fact she's been with other men; strange and unnecessary metaphors used to describe the climax. And there are many more.

When writing love scenes in short fiction, remember that desire and sexual response are based on emotion as well as physical action. Also remember that the majority of people develop sexual relations based on the old "first base, second base, third base, home" and do not skip a step in that progression. Read well-written romance at the same heat level you are writing and look for similarities and what works and what does not.

60   NANCY CASSIDY

PART SIX: KNOW YOUR MARKET

Who Reads Romance?

There are statistics available on the market share romance books receive. According to BookStats[12], the US Publishing Industry Annual Survey reported $27 billion in net revenue in 2013. And of that number, there was an estimated annual total sales value $1.08 billion in the romance genre! That represents approximately 13% of adult fiction.

According to the Romance Writers of America[13], "84% of the buyers of romance are women, and 41% of those women are 30–54 years old. And 35% have been buying romance for 20 years or more. Romance readers are highly represented in the South (USA) and those romance readers have an average annual income

---

[12] BookStats "a joint venture between the Association of American Publishers (AAP) and the Book Industry Study Group (BISG), is a first-of-its-kind data project with the goal of unifying the statistical model used throughout publishing, financial and media industries to track the size and shape of the U.S. publishing industry." **http://bookstats.org/bookstats.php**

[13] See this link for more on market research from Romance Writers of America **https://www.rwa.org/p/cm/ld/fid=580**

of $55,000. In reading vs. buying, 64% of these readers read romance more than once a month and 35% buy romance more than once a month."

Also we hear this from Romance Writers of America:

"**The Breakdown for Print is as follows:** romantic suspense (53%); contemporary romance (41%); historical romance (34%); erotic romance (33%); new ddult (26%); paranormal romance (19%); young adult romance (18%); and Christian romance (17%).

"**E-book: romantic suspense** (48%); contemporary romance (44%); erotic romance (42%); historical romance (33%); paranormal romance (30%); new adult (26%); young adult romance (18%); and Christian romance (14%)."

As of April, 2015, Amazon.com notes there are over 650,000 books listed as Books: Romance. And over 420,000 titles listed as Kindle: Romance. The number of available romance books exceeds every other genre, superseded only by general literature.

63

Who Reads Short Romance Stories – Serials, Novellas, Shorts, and Anthologies?

As established in the Brief History of Short Fiction section of this book, today's short fiction is most easily accessed through novellas and short stories sold electronically either as stand-alone novellas, collections of novellas (boxed sets), anthologies, or as parts of online magazines.

In a report by Bowker[14] regarding e-book reading and choice of reader he explains:

"Understanding device use is important as the survey reveals further correlation between device choice and genre preference, with certain fiction genres continuing to dominate on dedicated e-readers, while some specialized nonfiction genres perform better on other devices. For example, those who prefer dedicated e-readers were more likely to select general fiction, mystery, literary fiction, or romance as key e-book genres than users of other types of devices. How-to guides and manuals were more popular with those who

---

[14] Bowker Press Release April 5, 2013

prefer reading e-books on personal computers. Consumers who prefer e-reading via smartphones were more likely to read travel books than either tablet or dedicated e-reader users."

Why is this information important? With the predominant choice of genre readers still leaning toward dedicated e-readers (Kindle, Kobo, Nook), choice of distribution channels becomes clear: Amazon, Kobo Books, and Barnes and noble remain the top distributors. This is not to say iBookstore and other non-device specific distributors should be ignored by an author writing novellas, boxed sets, or anthologies, but it's clear that joining the bandwagon for device promotion is not a bad idea.

Looking at the largest e-book distributor, Amazon, there are over 77,670 books listed under Anthologies – Short Stories. This figure is up from 29,000 in 2009. The majority of these collections are by groups of authors rather than a single individual. Novellas seem harder to identify, but the numbers of books that qualify in this area are staggering as well.

Part Seven: Conclusion

The information in this book is laid out specifically for writers who wish to write compelling, short romantic fiction. This book offers you the information to consider before you start a new short piece, specifically using The Short Plot Method. It may take several attempts to write a professional, marketable, romantic short story, delivering a compelling beginning, middle, and end, with developed characters, and a full and rounded plot, complete with satisfying climax and ending. It takes practice to integrate the complex layers of story within tight word limitations.

You can do it.

Remember, that in order to tell a good story in a short timeframe, the plot must be simple and the characters understandable. And the story must evoke a depth of emotion and connection that keeps the story in the mind of the reader long after the pages are read. Plan to create short stories in ways that encourage readers to look for previous and next work of those authors. Romance readers love to read and they want to get the most out of the time they spend reading a book. Don't disappoint; give them reasons to leave their everyday lives and take time to read your books.

Take note of the statistics mentioned in the market information in the previous section of this book. It's impossible to keep up with fans' demands unless the novella and short story are incorporated into the savvy author's repertoire.

In the following appendices you will find the list of books that can explain in greater detail, the elements of GMC, POV, and more – and provide some agreed-upon best examples of short fiction. Please read on and, if you have questions or require support, you will contact the Red Pen Coach. You are encouraged to read the books that are listed as wonderful examples of short stories, and popular short stories in your choice of genre. Look for what works and apply it to your writing.

Also included is a list with a number of writing opportunities in which to practice The Short Plot Method. This list is also available on the Red Pen Coach website under the regularly updated Quickies page.

MORE ABOUT THE RED PEN COACH

We welcome you to ask questions and to visit us at **http://www.TheRedPenCoach.com**! We will be happy to see you there and hope to get to know you and to share your journey throughout your writing career.

The Red Pen Coach was created in 2011 by Nancy Cassidy – a multi-published author and freelance editor – to offer editing services to indie authors and small presses. In June of 2015, The Red Pen Coach happily grew, adding award-winning author, Donna Alward, to the editorial team.

Together, we offer editorial services to fiction writers of all genres with the exception of middle grade and picture books.

If you would like to know more about Nancy and her writing background, click the page **About Nancy.** To learn about Donna, click the page **About Donna.** Our rates and a complete description of our services can be found on the **Editing Services** page and the **Coaching Services** page on our website.

Want to hear what others think of work done by the RedPen Coach? Check out the **Testimonials** page.

Check **Author Resources** regularly for tips on writing, inspiration, and achieving your publishing goals.

APPENDIX A

Further Suggested Reading

For more on the history, art, and techniques you can apply to short stories, and for some fantastic examples of short fiction, here is some suggested reading:

1. *The Paris Review Presents The Art of the Short Story*
   http://www.amazon.com/Object-Lessons-Paris-Review-Presents-book/dp/B0089VSSUG
2. *The History of Short Stories in the Evening News*
   http://eveningnews.atwebpages.com/history1.htm
3. *Short Shorts: An Anthology of the Shortest Short Stories* (edited by Irving Howe and Ilana Wiener Howe) 1982
   http://www.amazon.com/Short-Shorts-Irving-Howe/dp/0553274406

*

For more on various writing techniques discussed in this book, consider the following books:

4. *GMC: Goal, Motivation and Conflict* by Debra Dixon
http://www.amazon.com/GMC-Motivation-Conflict-Debra-Dixon-ebook/dp/B00DZ01FRY

5. *Elements of Fiction Writing – Scene & Structure* by Jack Bickham
http://www.amazon.com/gp/product/B00D0AH01E

6. *The Emotion Thesaurus* (a great way to deepen POV with minimal use of words) by Angela Ackerman and Becca Puglisi
http://www.amazon.com/Emotion-Thesaurus-Writers-Character-Expression-ebook/dp/B00822WM2M

7. *On Writing Romance: How to Craft a Novel That Sells* by Leigh Michaels
http://www.amazon.com/Writing-Romance-Craft-Novel-Sells-ebook/dp/B00506WXDG

8. APPENDIX B:

Example of The Short Plot Method – Snow White and the Seven Dwarfs by Disney The Short Plot Method Plotting	
Title, Genre, Subgenre, Length:	Snow White, romance, paranormal, 20,000 words
Setting - Location:	Castle and the dwarfs' home in the woods
Setting - Length Of Time Covered:	Two months
Character Archetypes:	Innocent princess; brave prince; jealous witch
Trope:	soul mate/fate
One-liner:	Brave Prince Charming must save the innocent Snow White from her jealous stepmother/witch
Goals:	Prince – to bring justice (implies confrontation) Snow White – to live free (avoids confrontation)
Inciting Incident:	Prince spies the beautiful princess in the woods

One-liner:	Having escaped from her stepmother's assassin, Snow White seeks refuge with protective dwarfs and encounters the prince while dancing in the woods
Complication:	The witch discovers her assassin failed
One-liner:	The witch takes things into her own hands and poisons Snow White and only true love's kiss can wake the princess from a deathlike sleep
Climax:	The prince kisses Snow White
One-liner:	With a single kiss, Charming reveals that fate has chosen well – he loves the princess and she loves him – and Snow White awakens from the poison-apple spell
2nd Complication:	When Snow White survives, the witch goes mad
One-liner:	Transforming herself into a dragon to burn the woods and the princess, the witch can only be countered by pure bravery
2nd Climax	The prince kills the witch

(Optional):	
One-liner:	Charming slays the dragon in a mighty battle; Snow White becomes the queen
Anticlimax (Optional):	The dwarfs give their blessing
One-liner:	Although sorry to see their lady go, the dwarves, who had protected Snow White, bow to fate and arrange for the wedding
Happy Ending:	Snow White and Prince Charming are married and rule the land in peace

BLANK FORM	
The Short Plot Method Plotting	
Title, Genre, Subgenre, Length:	
Setting - Location:	
Setting - Length Of Time Covered:	
Character Archetypes:	
Trope:	
One-liner:	
Goals:	
Inciting Incident:	
One-liner:	
Complication:	
One-liner:	
Climax:	
One-liner:	
2nd Complication:	
One-liner:	
2nd Climax	

(Optional):	
One-liner:	
Anticlimax (Optional):	
One-liner:	
Happy Ending:	

*Note – *For a blank copy of this form please visit* http://www.theredpencoach.com/quickies

APPENDIX C

Current Short Fiction Opportunities, or Where to Look for Them

Short story publishing opportunities are constantly changing. Please review the submission guidelines for each company to ensure your story fits the correct length and theme. This list is also available at TheRedPenCoach.com where it is updated regularly.

*Note – *Before you agree to sell something to an online publication, be sure to investigate the publisher, as The Red Pen Coach cannot ensure the reputation or the quality of the publishers listed. Here is a great article on how to go about this investigation.*
http://www.writersrelief.com/blog/2010/04/online-literary-journals-how-to-determine-quality-and-reputation/[15]

---

[15] *This article (link) has been reprinted with the permission of* Writer's Relief, *an author's submission service that has been helping creative writers make submissions since 1994. Their work is highly recommended in the writing community, and there are TONS of freebies, publishing leads, and writers resources on their website. Check it out!*

ANTHOLOGIES

1. Meerkat Press (1k and up) – http://meerkatpress.com/submissions/
2. Ellora's Cave (10k ad up, some anthology work as well) – https://www.ellorascave.com/about-elloras-cave/write-for-ec/
3. Ravenous Romance (lengths vary and may include anthologies) – http://www.ravenousromance.com/general/submission-guidelines.php
4.

ONLINE MAGAZINES

1. *Fireside Fiction Company* – http://www.firesidefiction.com/submissions/
2. *Vestal Review* (Flash Fiction, 500 words) – http://www.vestalreview.org/guidelines/
3. *Timeless Tales Magazines* (Fairy Tales & Myths, Short Stories) – http://www.timelesstalesmagazine.com/#!submissions/c1vmu
4. *One Teen Story* (teen themes) – http://www.oneteenstory.com/index.php?page=submit
5. *Rattle* Single parent magazine (says poetry but they accept essays and short stories) – http://www.rattle.com/poetry/submissions/calls/
6. *Being a Grown-up* – Magazine on growing up –http://beingagrownupbook.blogspot.ca/

Novellas via E-Publishing Houses or E-First Houses

1. Riptide Publishing (LGBT, 15k and up) – http://riptidepublishing.com/call-for-submissions
2. Books To Go Now (10k and up) – http://bookstogonow.com/submissions/
3. Liquid Silver Books (10k and up) – http://www.lsbooks.com/submission-calls-w15.php
4. Totally Entwined (10k and up) – http://www.totallyboundpublishing.com/submissions/submission-calls/
5. Prizm Books (10k and up) – http://www.prizmbooks.com/specialcalls.html
6. Heroes and Heartbreakers (15k and up) – http://www.heroesandheartbreakers.com/page/submissions
7. Ellora's Cave (10k ad up, some anthology work as well) – https://www.ellorascave.com/about-elloras-cave/write-for-ec/
8. Solstice Publishing (lengths vary per imprint) https://solsticepublishing.submittable.com/submit
9. Ravenous Romance (lengths vary and may include anthologies) – http://www.ravenousromance.com/general/submission-guidelines.php

10. Siren – Bookstrand (20k and up) – http://www.sirenbookstrand.com/submissions/
11. Entangled – 15k min – http://www.entangledpublishing.com/submission-information/
12. Samhain Publishing – 12K minimum – https://www.samhainpublishing.com/static/write
13. Carina Press – 35K min – http://carinapress.com/blog/submission-guidelines/
14. Tirgearr Publishing – 20K min – http://www.tirgearrpublishing.com/submissions/submission-guidelines.htm
15. Wild Rose Publishing – 7.5K min – http://www.wildrosepublishing.com/maincatalog_v151/index.php?main_page=page&id=102

80   NANCY CASSIDY

INDEX

Active vs. passive

Strong writing, 48, 55, 57

Adding emotion, 47-51

Anthology

Length of story categorization, 17

Archetypes, 36, 37, 42

Avoiding clichés, 47, 55, 57-58

Black moment, 21, 23, 43, 45, 46

Body language

Strong writing, 50

Character growth, 24, 31

Christian romance

Subgenre of romance, 12

Climaxes

Short Plot Method, 19, 40, 44-46

Complications

Short Plot Method, xvii, 40, 44, 45

Concise, 40, 55-56

Contemporary romance

Subgenre of romance, 10

Dialogue, 15, 29-31, 35, 51

Dynamic characters, 31, 32

Erotic romance

Subgenre of romance, 12, 62

External action arc. *See* Story arc

First person

POV, 25-26

Five senses

Strong writing, 48

Flash Fiction 5

Length of story categorization, 17

Flashback

Pacing, 35

Foreshadowing

Pacing, 35

Gift book

Short story form, 1

Happy ever after. *See* HEA

Happy for now. *See* HFN

HEA, 8, 21

HFN, 8, 21

Historical romance

Subgenre of romance, 9, 10, 62

Inspiring yourself, 50

Introductions

Short Plot Method, 40

Layering, 47, 53

Mash-Ups

Subgenre of romance, 13

Memes, 22, 36, 39, 43, 53

New adult. *See* New adult romance

Subgenre of romance, 11

Non-verbal

dialogue, 28

Novel

Length of story categorization 16, 20, 41

Novelette

Length of story categorization, 17

Novella

Length of story categorization, 16, 17

Online magazines

Short story form, 5

Pacing, 34

Paranormal romance

Subgenre of romance, 10, 13

Perma-free

Marketing, 17

Point of view, 2, 24-26

POV

Point of view, 24-28, 50, 66

Precision writing, 55

Resolutions

Short Plot Method, 40, 45

Romance reading statistics, 61

84   NANCY CASSIDY

Romantic arc. *See* Story arc

Romantic suspense

Subgenre of romance, 11, 13

Rule of three, 53, 54

Scene-and-sequel, 34

Science fiction romance

Subgenre of romance, 11

Second person

POV, 26

Serial

Length of story categorization, 17, 19

Setting, 28, 29

Short Plot Method,40, 42, 45

Short story

Length of story categorization, 16

Short-short

Length of story categorization, 17

Short-short story

Short-short, 5

Speech tag, 30

Static characters, 31

Story arc, 20, 21, 25

Symbolism,47, 53, 54

Tense

POV, 24, 27

Themes, 36-38
Third person
  POV, 26
Tropes, 36-38
Word choices
  Strong writing, 48
Young adult
  Subgenre of romance, 12, 15, 62

ABOUT THE AUTHOR

After achieving a business degree with a double major in management and marketing, and after years of writing technical sales proposals, Nancy Cassidy decided to bring the passion she felt about books to a more public level, and follow her writing dreams.

Fourteen years ago, she joined the Romance Writers of America and the Romance Writers of Atlantic Canada, and began writing romance. Eventually, thanks to some wonderful editors, she learned what made a story work.

In the spring of 2011, Nancy began a year-long, distance internship with top New York literary agency, The Bent Agency. She spent her time there as a romance specialist, reviewing queries and manuscripts. It's a fascinating side of the publishing business!

In August 2011, Nancy opened TheRedPenCoach.com and began editing all genres of fiction, with the exception of picture books or middle grade fiction. She has worked with over sixty novels from small presses and indie authors.